Travel and Vacation Advertising Cuts
from the Twenties and Thirties

EDITED BY

T<small>RINA</small> R<small>OBBINS</small> <small>AND</small> C<small>ASEY</small> R<small>OBBINS</small>

DOVER PUBLICATIONS, INC.
New York

Publisher's Note

The 1920s and 1930s saw an unprecedented flourishing of black-and-white print advertising art. In styles ranging from the elegant Art Deco of the affluent to the grotesque "lowbrow" caricatures of mail-order novelty catalogs, countless anonymous artists created a wealth of illustration that is today cherished for its directness and stylistic flair. This book contains 600 cuts focusing on travel and vacation themes from this golden age of advertising art, and serves both as an overview of this important era as well as a convenient resource for present-day graphic artists.

Copyright

Copyright © 1994 by Dover Publications, Inc.
All rights reserved under Pan American and International Copyright Conventions.

Published in Canada by General Publishing Company, Ltd., 30 Lesmill Road, Don Mills, Toronto,

Bibliographical Note

Travel and Vacation Advertising Cuts from the Twenties and Thirties is a new work, first published by Dover Publications, Inc., in 1994.

DOVER *Pictorial Archive* SERIES

This book belongs to the Dover Pictorial Archive Series. You may use the designs and illustrations for graphics and crafts applications, free and without special permission, provided that you include no more than ten in the same publication or project. (For permission for additional use, please write to: Permissions Department, Dover Publications, Inc., 180 Varick Street, New York, N.Y. 10014.)

However, republication or reproduction of any illustration by any other graphic service, whether it be in a book or in any other design resource, is strictly prohibited.

Library of Congress Cataloging-in-Publication Data

Travel and vacation advertising cuts from the twenties and thirties / edited by Trina Robbins and Casey Robbins.
    p.   cm. — (Dover pictorial archive series)
    ISBN 0-486-28199-X (pbk.)
    1. Commercial art—History—20th century. 2. Tourist trade in art. I. Robbins, Trina.
II. Robbins, Casey. III. Series.
NC998.4.T73 1994
741.6'7—dc20
                                       94–13334
                                         CIP

Manufactured in the United States of America
Dover Publications, Inc., 31 East 2nd Street, Mineola, N.Y. 11501

Vacation

going away

"across the Atlantic"

ORIENT

WORLD CRUISE

*Discovery
Tours to
the Islands of
mystery
and charm*

SOUTH SEAS—
Islands of Romance

"The Voyage of Your Dreams"

THE Ojib'way
IN THE HEART OF GEORGIAN BAY

Britain from the World's most Famous Train

Travel by Motor Stage

Safely   Comfortably

A Cruise
ROUND THE WORLD
including the
SOUTH SEA ISLANDS

MOST COMPLETE CRUISE OF THE
MEDITERRANEAN

NASSAU

"Where shall we stay?"

Direct from the Sea

College Inn

WINTER INEXPENSIVELY
ON TROPIC
TREASURE ISLE . . .

SUNSET LIMITED
to California

Special Parking Service *at the Harbor*

—for passengers on the
super-express liners —

Look for the man who runs the "RED CROWN" PUMP

GASOLINE

Take a Trip this Fall
THROUGH OLD **NEW HAMPSHIRE**
The Friendly State

Homeland
of Beauty
Industry
and
Agriculture

R.S.V.P.

Healthy
recreation
in sunny **TUCSON!**

- on your way
to or from
California
take the

Indian-detour

Scenic Cruises to and from
CALIFORNIA

5000 Miles of Scenic Beauty

On the Rock Island's great loop tour of the West —

Colorado
Yellowstone
California

Vermont
fits your budget

PACIFIC NORTHWEST

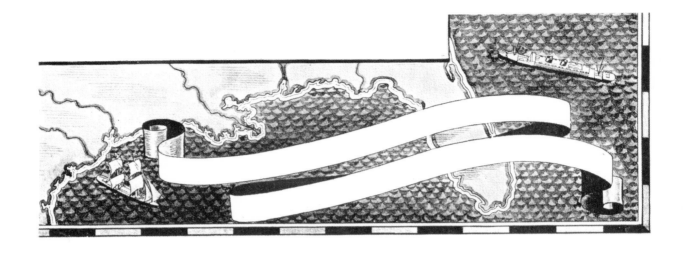

New Ocean House

DIRECTLY ON THE OCEAN

San Diego
California

REVELATION

SUITCASE

ADJUSTS TO 14 SIZES

YELLOWSTONE PARK LINE

A Ranch
Vacation

*This
Summer?*

THUNDERING
...the waterfalls in
YOSEMITE
NATIONAL PARK

Save for Seattle!

Overnight from San Francisco or Los Angeles

On *every* trip West!
YOSEMITE
NATIONAL PARK

THE PORTLAND ROSE AT MULTNOMAH FALLS

All-Steel Trains to New York

THE BEST WAY ANY DAY

Maine

VACATIONS
FOR SALE
CHEAP!

in the

WEST

*A Night Afloat
On A Wonder Boat!*
To LOS ANGELES

niagara
to the
sea

LOS ANGELES

South With the Sun
to SAN ANTONIO

There's Sunshine
all Winter in
TUCSON

NOW! TAKE THIS LOW-PRICED OUTING

2 DAYS $10 Big Bear

Golfing
Fishing
Touring
Boating
Tennis
Sports

Make Jacksonville Florida, Your Winter Playground

NO CALIFORNIA TRIP IS COMPLETE WITHOUT YOSEMITE

AIRCRAFT PARTS FOR TODAY'S AND TOMORROW'S FLYING

Florida *and the* SUNNY SOUTH

FLORIDA MAGIC NIGHTS!
BATHING BEAUTIES!
FASHIONABLE MIAMI!

"The PALM BEACH GIRL"

PEP AND SPEED
BRIGHT AND BREEZY!
HAPPY·SNAPPY FUN!

COME UP TO
ASHEVILLE
NORTH CAROLINA
IN THE LAND OF THE SKY
ALL OUT DOOR SPORTS
WRITE FOR LITERATURE
ASHEVILLE CHAMBER OF COMMERCE
ASHEVILLE, N.C.

Travel the D&C LAKE LINES
Great Lakes First!

SAN ANTONIO

~~old in years
~~ young in spirit!

California's Own

The standard of
coastwise
steamship
service

HARVARD   YALE

1
SCENIC CRUISES TO AND FROM

california
and New York

TEXAS AND MEXICO

Fares Cut Again!

COLORADO

BIENVENUE À QUÉBEC

Warm, dry *Sunshine*
–all Winter in
TUCSON

The
Indian·detour

on your way to California *this winter* be sure to take the

INDIAN·DETOUR

Warm, dry *Sunshine*
now~in
TUCSON

Sunny winter vacations
in the old haunts of the Conquistadors
TUCSON
("Too-sŏhn")

SAVE FOR SEATTLE

• **THIS**
IS
Bargain
Year

OUT
WEST

Vacation
Costs are
Lowest in Years

SBy**EA**
the
delightful
way

between
New York
and
CALIFORNIA

PLAY
TENNIS...GOLF
in warm mid-winter sunshine

Treasure Isle Beckons

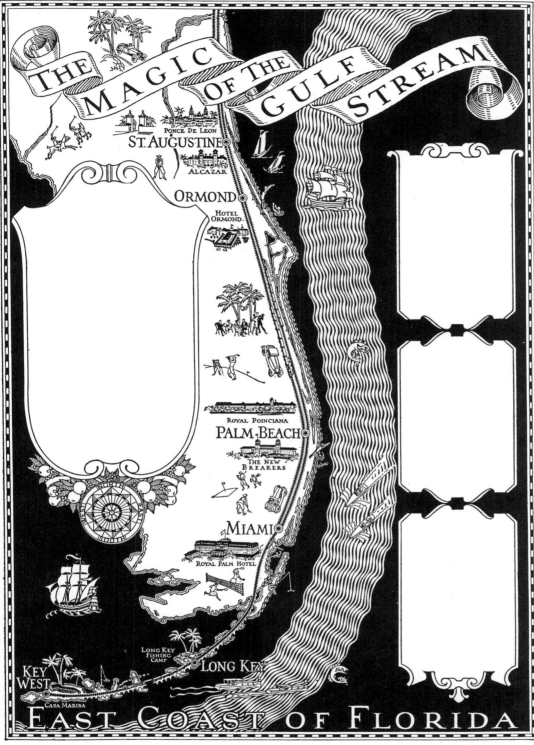

THE MAGIC OF THE GULF STREAM

PONCE DE LEON
ST. AUGUSTINE
ALCAZAR

ORMOND
HOTEL ORMOND

ROYAL POINCIANA
PALM BEACH
THE NEW BREAKERS

MIAMI
ROYAL PALM HOTEL

LONG KEY FISHING CAMP
LONG KEY

KEY WEST
CASA MARINA

EAST COAST OF FLORIDA

Scenic Cruises To CALIFORNIA via "Spanish Americas"

ASHEVILLE
NORTH CAROLINA
Its season is "All the year Round!"

Polish up the old golf clubs if you're going to Asheville

Why St.Louis Grows

"Chequing" the American Traveler

A million miles of *sunshine* in
TUCSON
("Too-sóhn")

Make Your "1" this Winter in
DAYTONA BEACH
Florida

Mackinac Is.

GREAT LAKES Pleasure Ports

Niagara Falls

D&C LAKE LINES

Come! Bring the Family

MINNESOTA
welcomes YOU

Come and play to your heart's content. Many a thrill awaits you.

LAND OF
Ten Thousand
LAKES

What I think of
Maine

VACATION TRIPS BY SEA
Only $12 to San Francisco
$29.50 to Portland
FIRST CLASS

ALASKA

TO THE
ORIENT
and
ROUND THE WORLD

COME UP TO
ASHEVILLE
N.C.
In the Land of the Sky

Towering Peaks-A Scenic
Wonderland-Superb Golf-
All Out Door Sports
Investment
Opportunities

FLORIDA AND CUBA

YELLOWSTONE

This winter enjoy
SUNNY LIVING!

Where it's Springtime all the Time

Clearwater
FLORIDA
West Coast on the Gulf

California
WHERE LIFE IS BETTER

The Sunshine City

*Resort Metropolis
of Florida's Gulf Coast*

NASSAU · MIAMI · HAVANA

28

this WINTER
play under
SUMMER PALMS
in
HAWAII

SOUTH SEAS
★ **HAWAII**
♣ **NEW ZEALAND**
○ **AUSTRALIA**
via bewitching Samoa and Fiji

ADVENTURE URGES · ECONOMY PERMITS
this autumn-gloried trip at reduced fares to

HAWAII

30

DISCOVER
AMERICA'S OWN
tropical paradise
HAWAII

Hanamalea
"the spirit of taking life easy"

Hawaii

Take a South
Sea Honeymoon
this autumn

Grow young again
in HAWAII

HAWAII

The **WORLD'S** *Enchanted Island Playground*

HAWAII
The
World's New
Island Playground

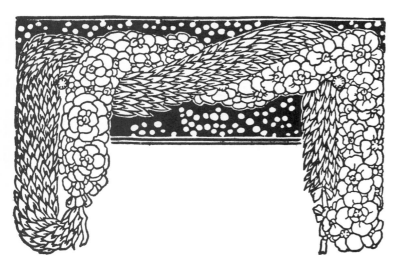

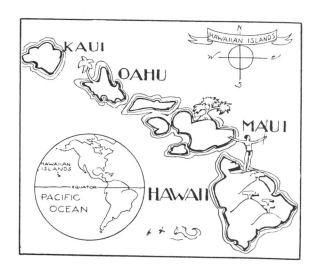

Spring Dawns in Tropic
Radiance in Hawaii···—

39

HAWAII
by a
different
route!

The "Magic Isles of the Pacific" may now be reached by a delightfully different route—the "Great Circle Route of Sunshine."

DIRECT *from* Los Angeles *to* Honolulu

Tired of the same old vacation rounds?

Then come to
HAWAII *~this time!*

HULA MOONS

HAWAII

for *The* MODERN ROBINSON CRUSOE

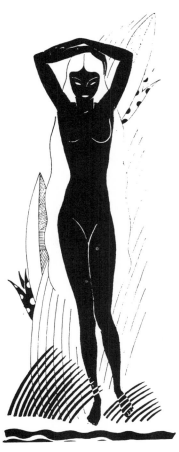

HAWAII

CAP HAITIEN
CARTAGENA
CURACAO
SAN JUAN
S.T. PIERRE
BARBADOS
PORT OF SPAIN
LA GUAYRA
NASSAU
ST. THOMAS
SANTO DOMINGO
PORT AU PRINCE
FORT DE FRANCE
HAVANA

HOW EASY
to see the
whole thrilling
world

Lucky!
to go to Europe
in the fall

All Expense Cruises!
HAVANA AND MEXICO CITY

HAVANA
by EXPRESS STEAMERS

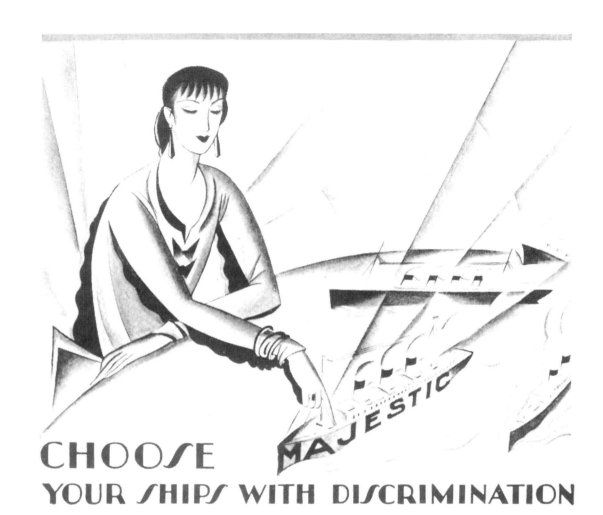

CHOOSE
YOUR SHIPS WITH DISCRIMINATION

Steamship Sailings

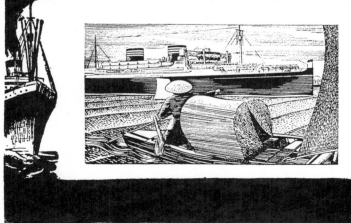

THROUGH A PORTHOLE
on the
HOMERIC

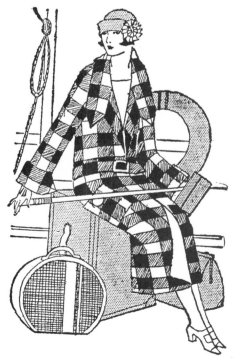

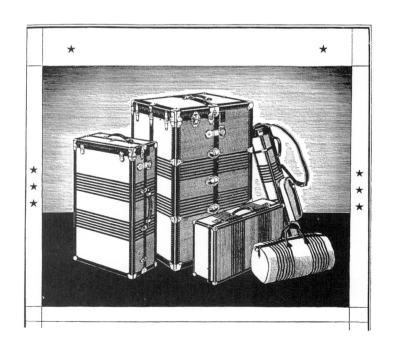

THE EUROPEAN TRAVEL SENSATION OF 1930!

EUROPE
in 7 Days of Solid Comfort by
STABILIZED SHIPS

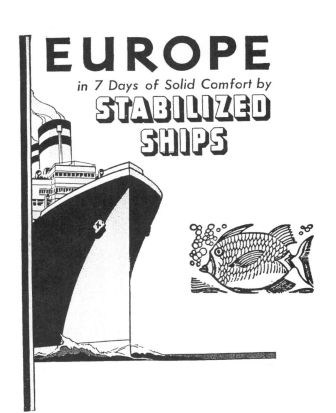

HAVANA

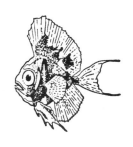

LUXURY
CRUISES

West Indies
Panama Canal

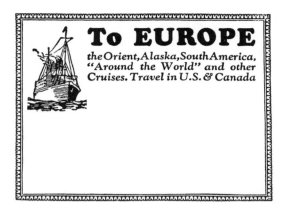

To EUROPE
the Orient, Alaska, South America, "Around the World" and other Cruises. Travel in U.S. & Canada

Under the
Southern Cross

A Tropic Paradise

SOUTH SEAS—
Islands of Romance

4 Mediterranean Winter Cruises

WEST INDIES
CRUISES on the delightful MEGANTIC

voyage
to vacation land on

The Best Time to Visit

SOUTH AMERICA!

The Luxury Cruise to the
Mediterranean
PALESTINE EGYPT

SARASOTA

EGYPT and the MEDITERRANEAN

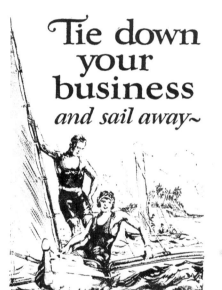

Tie down your business
and sail away~

to the
ISLAND of your DREAMS

Enjoy July and August in HAWAII

CRUISING
THE
SEVEN SEAS

Two de Luxe Cruises

From New York
Oct. 24, 1925

From San Francisco
Feb. 9, 1926

Los Angeles, Feb. 10

HAWAII	JAPAN
CHINA	BORNEO
PHILIPPINES	BURMA
SINGAPORE	JAVA
CEYLON	INDIA
EGYPT	ITALY
ALGERIA (or Riviera)	
MADEIRA	

54

SUNSET LIMITED

to California

Sunset Route

Scenic Cruises to
CALIFORNIA
via the Panama Canal
8
Visits in the
"SPANISH
AMERICAS"

56

Cruise to

NEW YORK

or Havana
via Panama

Autumn is Spring in Rio

WEST INDIES CRUISES

to SOUTH AMERICA

To the Orient

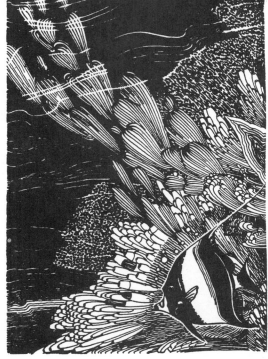

SOUTH
AMERICA

SOUTH
AMERICA
via
HAVANA
Panama—Peru
—Chile

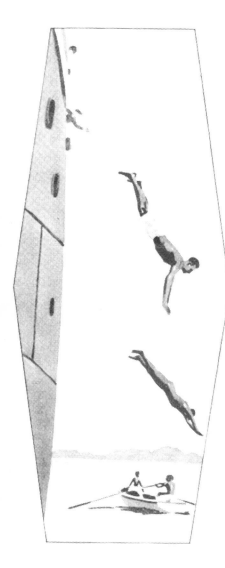

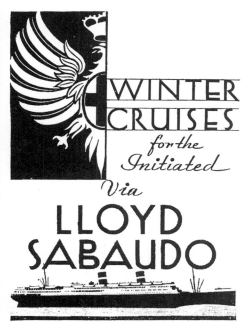

Cruises of Enchantment
WEST INDIES

WINTER CRUISES *for the Initiated Via*
LLOYD SABAUDO

WINTER
CRUISES
TO THE
West
Indies

Caribbean
Cruises

Your Ships
to the Orient

IN THE GARDEN OF ALLAH

5th Annual Cruise de Luxe

To the

MEDITERRANEAN

EGYPT – PALESTINE – NEAR EAST

'50th Anniversary'
Cruise de Luxe

TO THE **Mediterranean**

WORLD CRUISE

ON A VOYAGE
OF 132 DAYS
129 WERE SUNNY

THE LUXURY CRUISE
TO THE
MEDITERRANEAN
PALESTINE ≠ EGYPT
Leaving New York
FEB. 6th, 1924

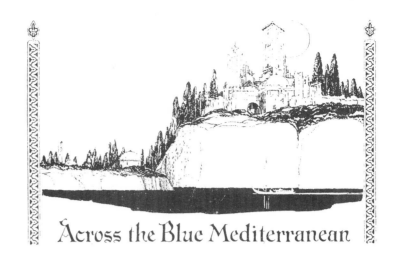

Across the Blue Mediterranean

THE DELUXE
MEDITERRANEAN
CRUISE

Egypt *and the* Mediterranean

Voyages Modernes

COOL

HAWAII

EUROPE

The
CRUISE OF 1928

SOUTH AMERICA
AFRICA
MEDITERRANEAN ▴ EUROPE

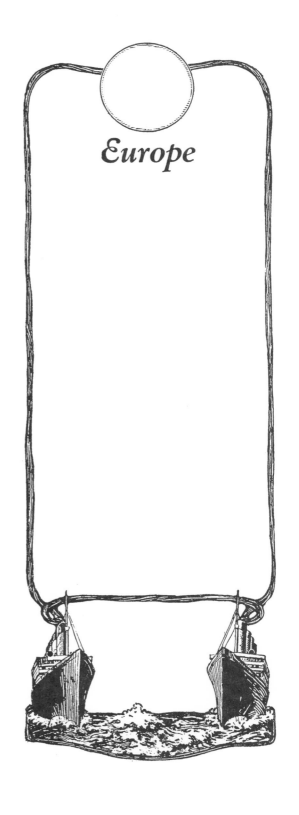

Europe

THE CRUISES SUPREME

to the MEDITERRANEAN

Madagascar in the Indian Ocean—island of jungle-smothered villages, smiling Malagasies, palm-fringed shores and strange native dhows—unknown to other cruises—is on the route of

Round Africa Cruise

Second Great African Cruise

Shakespeare's Land.

Pre-arranged Comfort
on your trip in Europe

HEY! Want to make friends easily? Let 'em know you're connected with **AVIATION!**

1928-29 Cruises

Fastest
Time
Finest
Ships

South
America

Two WORLD CRUISES

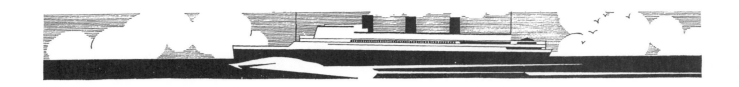

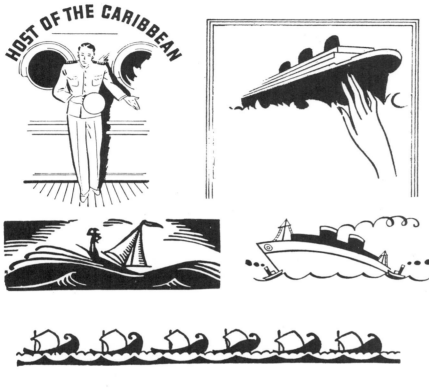

HOST OF THE CARIBBEAN

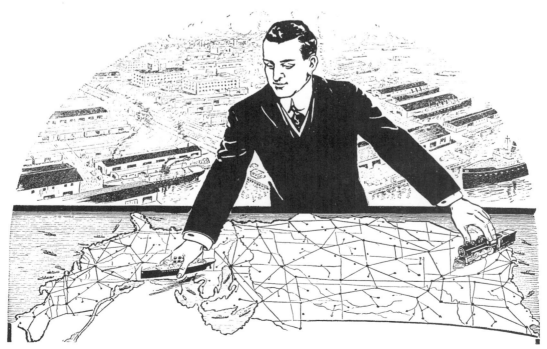

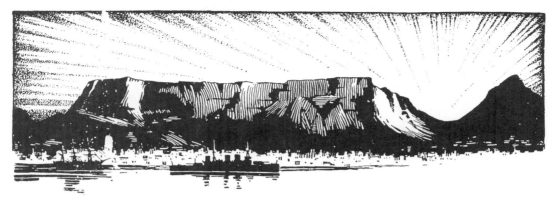

A cruise for true travelers—to lands and cities far from the worn routes of travel

TO EUROPE

Travel "Cabin" . . . the modern way to Europe!

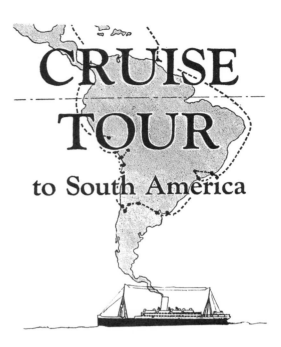

CRUISE TOUR
to South America

THE LUXURY CRUISES
West Indies
Panama Canal

LUXURY CRUISE
Mediterranean
PALESTINE
EGYPT

See Old Mexico
from El Paso
6 *minutes away!*
6¢ *car fare!*

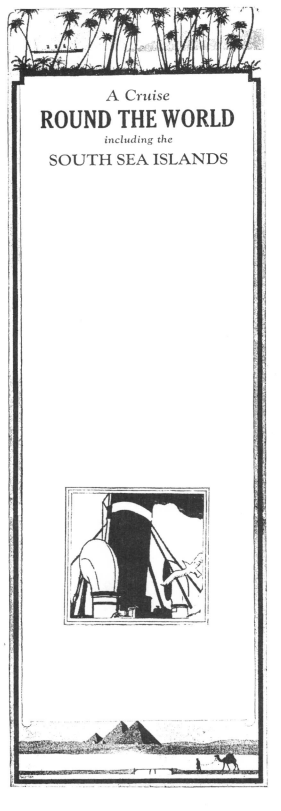

A Cruise
ROUND THE WORLD
including the
SOUTH SEA ISLANDS

EUROPE !

Are they just names on a map to **YOU** ?

Pre-arranged Comfort

on your trip in Europe

RUSSIA - (MOSCOW AND LENINGRAD)

SPRING—IN THE MEDITERRANEAN

CHANGE YOUR MIND

GIVE IT
NEW BEAUTY
NEW INTERESTS
AND NEW EXPERIENCES

In the Welsh Tyrol

CANADA...*an Old World Near at Hand*

Via Honolulu
to the
ORIENT

Travel over the Sunshine Belt

AROUND THE WORLD
in 80 HOURS

RAYMOND-WHITCOMB

Round the World
• Cruise •

TOP O' THE WORLD CLUB
GREEN VALLEY LAKE

TEMPLE TOURS

Make Travel Mean More

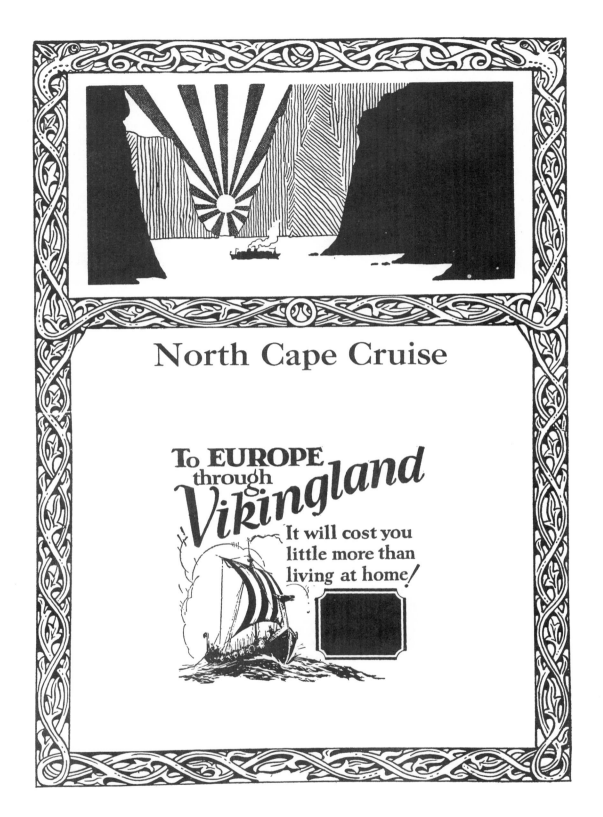

North Cape Cruise

To **EUROPE** through *Vikingland*

It will cost you little more than living at home!

EUROPE
INDEPENDENT TOURS

West Indies Cruises

Morro Castle, Havana

CUBA PORTO RICO PANAMA JAMAICA VIRGIN ISLANDS CURACAO
NASSAU   BARBADOS   TRINIDAD   VENEZUELA   MARTINIQUE
Fascinating bits of the Old World that lie on the warm Caribbean

For the short trip or the world tour ~ Baggage Insurance

Eliminate Travel Worry

Of all travel possibilities, the trip which encircles the globe is incomparably the most interesting & memorable.

Round the World Cruise

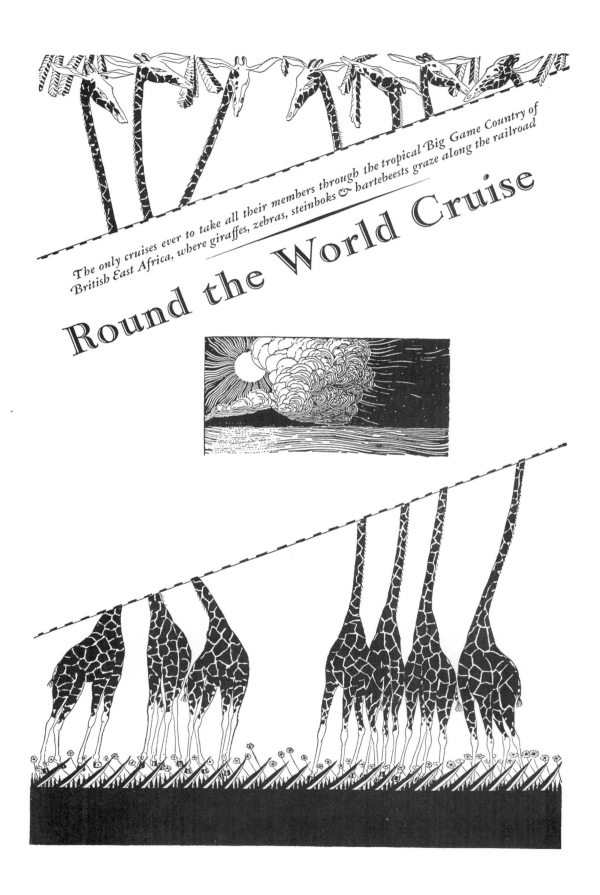

The only cruises ever to take all their members through the tropical Big Game Country of British East Africa, where giraffes, zebras, steinboks & hartebeests graze along the railroad

Round the World Cruise

When
an American
goes to Europe

York--
the Jewel of England

ENGLAND
the daily pageant

SCOTLAND
& IRELAND
an ever-changing pageant

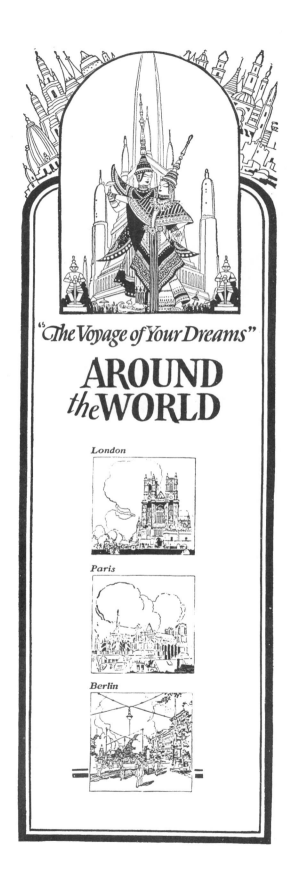
86

GLASGOW is the front door of Europe

Will you go to EUROPE

this comfortable carefree way?

FROM **NEW YORK** to **EUROPE** via **NORTH CAPE** and **MIDNIGHT SUN LAND**

Play Santa Claus!
Give Yourself This

All-Expense Trip to Europe

37 Days for $385.00

SEE
England
Holland
Belgium
France

VISIT
London
Stratford
Oxford
Amsterdam
The Hague
Brussels
Paris
and other points
of interest

FREE
TOUR
BOOK

L M S

LONDON MIDLAND & SCOTTISH
RAILWAY OF GREAT BRITAIN

England

for the best vacation in Europe

To the MEDITERRANEAN
EGYPT – PALESTINE – NEAR EAST

SEE THE HISTORY OF
BRITAIN

EUROPE
All Expenses
$334

See
SCOTLAND
ENGLAND
HOLLAND
BELGIUM
GERMANY
FRANCE
in 30 Days

THE MEDITERRANEAN
+ AND RUSSIA +

A NEW CRUISE

*The
Best way
to see
Gt. Britain*

To the heart of the Orient in two weeks

Orient

Another Cruise
Around the World

MEDITERRANEAN

Near East
Egypt   Holy Land

and practically Every Port of Historic and Romantic Interest

THE 1928-29 WORLD CRUISE OF THE BELGENLAND

Largest, finest liner ever to circle the globe

"The Voyage of Your Dreams"

NEW FAST SISTER MOTORSHIPS

ACROSS THE ATLANTIC

ENGLAND   IRELAND
FRANCE   GERMANY

...MEET A BEEFEATER.....TACKLE AN ALP.....QUAFF A LÖWENBRÄU....

LOUVRE A LITTLE...FEATHER YOUR CAP IN THE TYROL..SHOP THE PONTE VECCHIO

KISS THE BLARNEY STONE...HIKE THE DYKES..STEP OUT AFTER DARK IN BERLIN